To be had at the Canning Library, College Street, Calcutta.

THE

OVERSTRAIN IN EDUCATION

BY

R. A. ARMSTRONG, B.A.

[*Reprinted from* THE MODERN REVIEW, *April*, 1883.]

London :

JAMES CLARKE & CO., 13 & 14, FLEET STREET.

Price Sixpence.

THE OVERSTRAIN IN EDUCATION.

ON entering the Dome Saloon of the New Capitoline Museum, at Rome, the visitor may see on his left-hand side the tombstone of one Q. Sulpicius Maximus. The subject of this monument was no hero of the camp or of the Senate, but a little fellow not twelve years old whose title to fame was the defeat of fifty-two competitors in the improvisation of Greek verses. Specimens of his pretty skill are graven on the marble. But the pathetic epitaph relates that death was the price of the over-stimulation of the boyish brain.

Such, so far as I know, outside China, was the first case of death from competitive examination. When will be the last?

No Englishman can fail to feel some pride in the extraordinary advance which the last quarter-of-a-century has seen in the education of the English people. The purpose of this article is to show that that advance has not been wholly in the right direction, and that it has not been without grave drawbacks. But he would indeed be a one-sided critic who should not confess that great and good things have been done. The average number of children in attendance at primary schools in Great Britain in 1857 was 626,696; in 1881 it was 3,273,501. In other words, the increase was five-fold, while the growth in population was but an addition of one-third. In 1857, one in thirty-five and a-half of the population was at a primary school; in 1881, one in nine. Whatever else this means, it means an enormous diffusion of the primary arts of civilisation—reading, writing, arithmetic; it means also a vast conversion of savagery into orderly decorum. At the same time the spread of the higher education has proceeded at no less extraordinary a pace—at any rate among girls and women. "Fair girl graduates" are no longer a poet's half-humorous dream, but sober fact. In every large town the new Girl's High School vies with the old foundation of the Grammar School which has been usurped by boys. Young ladies may now know chemistry as well as talk botany, and we no longer marvel at her quaintness when we read that Lady Jane Grey loved Greek and Latin. Liverpool, Birmingham, Leeds, Sheffield, Bristol, Nottingham, as well as Manchester, are the seats of large and flourishing colleges, staffed with talented professors and richly endowed by the public spirit or the private munificence of their citizens.

But there is a dark side to the picture. All those millions go to school; but are they all educated? What is the general tone and strain of our educational leaders? In what direction do they point the aspirations of teacher and taught? In nine speeches or articles out of ten the one string harped upon is industrial success. Our young are to learn because otherwise the foreign competitor will beat them. Moral apologues by the thousand fall on our ears, the end and aim of which is "success in life"; and success in life means solely and simply getting plenty of money. Education is preached by the great chorus of its preachers as a commodity of mercantile value; and so, after all, it is not education that is preached, but sheer technical training, from first to last.

The first great apostle of the modern educational movement in this country was Mr. Robert Lowe. Lord Sherbrooke breathes now a serene atmosphere, and his cynicism may have risen to a higher level. But the Mr. Lowe of the old days was a philosopher who had one safe measure for all men, and that was money. It is not yet five years since he wrote: " Once place a man's ear within the ring of pounds, shillings, and pence, and his conduct can be counted on with the greatest nicety."* Such was the avowed

* "Recent Attacks on Political Economy." *Nineteenth Century* November, 1878, p. 864.

principle of the able man to whom, by an unhappy fate, was consigned the guidance of the movement at the moment when the British people were first aroused to the conviction that something big must be done in education. The famous Code of 1861 was the issue : and that Code set firm upon its pedestal the idol " payment by results." The simple social philosophy propounded by Mr. Lowe penetrated every wheel and screw of the new educational machinery. His desire was to govern the conduct of teachers, so he rattled pounds, shillings, and pence at their ears. His whole reliance was on their pecuniary avidity : to their sense of the noble character of their task and its pregnant issues he made no appeal whatever. For he himself has said that where the money-motive once comes in, men's " deviations from a line of conduct which can be foreseen and predicted, are so slight that they may practically be considered as non-existent." *

Nor was the public sentiment on the whole at all averse to the clever minister's expedient for getting good results from the educational institutions of the country. The children were to be educated that they might themselves earn the more money by-and-by, and so increase the wealth of the nation : what more fitting than that the nation should put its investment into the most direct form possible, and pay the teacher so many shillings down for every boy he could turn out that could write a commercial letter and add up a page of ledger? The state was buying clerks and traders ; why not make the transaction between the state and the teacher who turned them out clear and simple, by promising him so many pounds a gross?

" Payment by results " is the very key of the whole commercial system of the modern world ; and commerce is the breath of the British citizen. Nothing could be more natural than its application to the new trade in which he was embarking—the trade which in 1870 was taken over as a national concern. The consequence has been, as in all cases where money is freely introduced into the market, an im-

* *Ibid.*, p. 864.

mense stimulus to production. The article demanded is delivered in ample quantities in spite of a few " spoils " in the shape of enfeebled bodies or shattered brains. And merchants, manufacturers, and Her Majesty's Ministers congratulate one another all round.

But how has the system acted on the men and women who are the chief agents in working it out ? No one who has at all acquainted himself with the actual work of our Elementary Schools can remain unimpressed by the large amount of conscientious, disinterested, and devoted work which many teachers carry on. Hundreds of them place before them as their foremost object, the welfare of the children entrusted to their care ; and I desire at the outset to express my profound respect for the numerous men and women whom the bribery of no Code can decoy from that method which they deem alone consonant with the physical, mental, and moral welfare of their scholars. But the bribes dangled before the eyes of the forty thousand Certificated Teachers of Great Britain * are constant and alluring ; and they are bribes offered to a class of persons worse paid, relatively to the services required of them, than any other whatsoever. † The livelihood of the teacher depends directly or indirectly on the percentage of children he can push through the ordeal of examination, and the number of subjects he can crowd into their brains. It is true that it is a common thing for Boards or Managers themselves to take the risk of this from year to year, and to pay the teacher a stipend not nominally based on his examination successes. But indirectly, save in the case of exceptionally wise authorities, the working is the same. If the grant earned falls, the stipend will be reduced, or the teacher will receive his dismissal.

Under the stimulus of this system of " payment by

* In 1881, England and Wales, 33,562 ; Scotland, 5,544. *Report of Com. of Council on Education*, p. xlv.

† " In 1870, the average salary was £95 for males, and £57 for females ; now it has risen to £121 for males, and £72 for females." *Presidential Address of Mr. R. Sykes at the annual conference of the National Union of Elementary Teachers*, 1882.

results," the average teacher has, for the past twenty years, been pressing his scholars for more and more remunerative response to his instruction. The motive appealed to by Mr. Lowe has been successfully brought into full and constant play, till in the minds of many it has outdone all others. Exceptionally able and ambitious teachers have driven their schools even harder than their neighbours, and have obtained results from which golden grants have flowed in, which have delighted managers and perhaps a little astonished " my lords." " My lords " have responded by screwing up the conditions of grants to a higher and higher pitch; and so the stimulus to the average teacher has grown more and more goading from Code to Code.

It is then, in the interests of both scholars and teachers, a question for urgent inquiry whether this process has or has not resulted in an excessive nervous strain upon the teacher. I say in the interest of scholar as well as of teacher, because there is no profession in which nervous strain must be so ruinous to the quality of the work done as that of the pedagogue. The overtaxed barrister may lay up for himself paralysis or lunacy; yet while he is still able to stick to his work, the strain on his nerves will only make his cross-examinations a little sharper, and his references to his " learned friend" a trifle more acid. The overtaxed preacher may, if he is an earnest one, preach morbid sermons with a false strain of sentiment running through them; yet his hearers will for the most part be proof against his appeals, and rather raise their eyebrows in surprise at his exaggerated expressions than set to work to shape their lives according to his views. But the overtaxed school-teacher becomes thereby hopelessly incapable of that just balance of firmness and kindness, that happy admixture of patience, energy, and cheerfulness, which is of more importance to the conduct of his school than any certificate or the praise of any inspector. Hence the question how the nervous systems of the teaching fraternity are affected by the pressure of successive Codes is a question of unsurpassed moment in estimating our national education.

Such an inquiry is indeed beset with difficulty. Official statistics are impossible to obtain. The Committee of Council on Education duly report the number of teachers with whom they deal, and the figure of the grants they earn ; but they have no column to show the prevalence of depression of physique or the percentage of lives sacrificed in the fierceness of the competition. I have, however, made it my business to acquaint myself, by correspondence or conversation, with the experience of a large number of head-teachers on this and other points. I have selected some of these on the ground of facility of personal access to them, others because I was specially recommended to them on account of their width or length of experience, others quite casually and without any previous knowledge whatever, picking the names of their schools out of the official list of Elementary Schools aided by Parliamentary grants. Of those of whose views I have thus had the opportunity of informing myself, more than seventy per cent. believe that they themselves or members of their staff have suffered in health from the pressure of the Code requirements, and many add striking testimony concerning other members of the profession, of whose breakdown they have had personal knowledge. Some of the statements which have reached me deserve a more special reference. The head-master of a brilliantly successful British school in Liverpool writes to me that, though he is enthusiastically fond of his work, he is, at thirty-nine, prematurely grey, and has undergone a surgical operation for a disease brought on by over-work. He suffers greatly from indigestion, especially just before inspection ; and he adds that the master of a neighbouring school died of disease of the heart, at the age of forty-two, brought on, in the words of his physician, " by the worries and anxieties of school-work." " Only those," says the head-master of one of the largest Board schools in the East of London, " who know the anxiety of the teacher for a few weeks before the inspection can fully enter into the strain upon the mind, the excessive nervousness and even sometimes irritability caused by the desire to do well or

inspection day." The teacher of a Church school in a thriving Midland town tells me, " I have often been taken for fifty and am not yet forty years old ; two years ago I had to exercise the greatest care, or the doctor said the mind would collapse." The late head-master of the excellent Lower Moseley-street Schools, Manchester, mentions two teachers of his acquaintance, both of whom were paralysed, and says that they always attributed their breakdown to the harassing and unyielding conditions of the Code regulations, combined perhaps with the constant inhalation of a vitiated air. " My medical adviser," says a Bristol teacher, " has distinctly warned me of the result of this pressure, going so far as to assert that, if not stopped, I should materially shorten my days." A teacher formerly very eminent in his own town, now at rest in the well-earned haven of a country rectory, looking back on the days of struggle with the Code, writes to me in a very careful communication, " With all the care I could exercise by the use of the usual means for preserving one's health—and my constitution, I believe, was an exceptionally strong one—I suffered from frequent attacks of biliousness, and twice, at the critical time of the inspection, my health quite gave way, owing to nothing but the constant mental and bodily strain, in an impure atmosphere, notwithstanding everything was done that could be done in the way of efficient ventilation. Two promising young men, assistant masters, who had been pupil teachers, died of consumption, according to my belief, from too close application, and I reckoned on one or more pupil-teachers being away from their duty from sickness in other parts of the year beside the usual holidays." A country head-master complains that his health is undermined by the strain involved in conducting a class consisting of Standards IV., V., VI., and VII. all together. " I have," says he, "four divisions in the class all doing different work at the same time in arithmetic, and three in dictation. I must dictate to Standard IV, read a tale twice over to Standard V., and superintend a theme or letter for Standards

VI. and VII." Such a school, it will be said, is miserably under-staffed. It is true ; but it is staffed in perfect accordance with Government requirements. A friend of my own, whose school stands foremost in its town for the business aptitude of the boys it turns out year by year—where, indeed, a regular list is kept of applications for scholars from employers—has been at the pains to place in my hands a statement which derives great weight from his long and wide experience. In the course of a review of the effects of the system on the physique of teachers, he says, "the nervous power of the digestive organs fails first generally. Head affections prevail. Paralysis, apoplexy, dementia supervene. Were it possible to get at the vital statistics of the great body of certificated teachers during the last twenty-five years, a sad history would be revealed. I judge of the mass from my actual knowledge of seven teachers whom I knew best during my college-life. Of the seven, only two survive" —my friend is, I suppose, five-and-forty years of age—" and these have had, since passing their fortieth year, very severe and protracted illnesses. Their lives are no longer such as a careful insurance office would accept at ordinary rates. Nor can an opinion on this point be founded safely on the cases of teachers now at work in schools. It is notorious that those who can escape from the profession, do so. Nothing is more painful than to find teachers occupying good situations, so far as salary is concerned, bent on getting away from the work if they can."

Probably the record among the mistresses would prove a still sadder one than that of the masters ; though I am inclined to think that it would be modified by the fact that the females are knocked out of the race at an earlier stage in their career than the males. A few days since a successful mistress told me of one after another of her successive pupil-teachers who had found their way to the asylum or otherwise utterly collapsed. She herself suffers acutely from chronic nerve-strain, and describes how at night, not sleeping, but awake, she will enter into some explanation to her pupil-teacher, to find after many minutes that there is no pupil-teacher there, and that it is the walls of her chamber, not those of the schoolroom, that surround her. An accomplished head-mistress, in Suffolk, tells how the working up for examination is " the old man " on the teacher's back. " After the honest work of nine months," says she, " and the overstrain of the three in which the examination falls, I often feel as if I had been put upon the rack—bruised and sore in body as well as in mind. About five years ago I had a complete break-down, when I became very deaf, and my memory seemed suddenly to have forsaken me. A long rest restored the hearing, but the memory has never regained its old power. . . . I assure you that, in the quarter before the examination, I hold *all* my scholars individually in mind. A's spelling must be improved; B's arithmetic is weak; C is not perfect with her repetition, and so on. When I go to bed, there is still the same array of children to torment me in my sleep. Add, that I go to bed at twelve and rise at six to correct exercises, &c., and you may judge that the Code is a heavy burden."

The mortality among school-teachers, according to the *Schoolmaster*, amounts to 2 per cent. per annum, as against ½ per cent. among police and sailors. Of the recent students of a large normal college more than one in fifty has died each year, while the normal average mortality among persons between twenty-two and thirty-four years of age is less than one in a hundred.

But in 1881 there were in England and Wales 33,639 pupil teachers assisting the 33,562 certificated teachers. Perhaps these young people show a better bill of health, and we may turn to them for encouragement. I fear not. The pressure on these young lads and undeveloped girls is, if possible, more severe than that on the chiefs themselves. The five best hours of each of five days in the week are given by them to the labour of teaching, probably even more arduous to them, considering their inexperience and inefficiency, than to their overseers. It is to be hoped that Mr. Mundella's new clause limiting their hours of teaching-service to twenty-five per week may be so interpreted as to free them from the heartless drudgery of playing police over the " kept-in " out of school-hours day after day. But, even so, hard indeed is the life of these children, who, it must be remembered, may be bound at fourteen and practically even at thirteen years of age ; and Diocesan or Board requirements of the most burdensome character are too often added to those of the Department itself. A London master says that his pupil-teachers have no recreation whatever, except, perhaps, half-an-hour after tea. " On Saturdays," he explains, " lectures on Diocesan work have to be attended and Diocesan studies entered into ; drawing, science, &c., have to be done on this day. I hear everywhere the complaints of pupil-teachers and of those who have been pupil-teachers : their life is one of continual drudgery." The master of a very large Board School in the Midlands says, " I am engaged to take the classes in the pupil-teacher central scheme. These pupil-teachers attend two nights a week, from 6.30 to 8.30, and one night from 6.30 to 9 p.m. If, besides this, they attend any science-class or instruction in French or other language—as they must to get a good start at the Training College—and work up to it, I do not see where the time for recreation is to come from. As a matter of fact, the pupil-teachers who work hardest in school teaching, and who are, therefore, often the best teachers *restore the balance by neglect of systematic study.*" This is the London Board's pupil-teacher's Saturday, according to a twenty-five years' head-master: " A pupil-teacher leaves home at 8.30, attends lectures from 9 to 12.30, then has four hours' hard study to prepare his lessons for the various tutors for Monday, when he again goes to the Centre from 6 to 8.30 p.m. If we break down, whose fault is it, but that of the powers that be—the Taskmasters ? " " I fear," says Miss Müller, of the London School Board, " there is very little doubt that the majority of school-mistresses and all pupil-teachers live in a state of ceaseless mental worry, which is injurious to health and perfectly incompatible with that happy and calm temper that every one has a right to enjoy whose life is well-ordered and properly balanced."*

* Report of the National Union of Elementary Teachers, 1882. P. lxxxiii.

But it will be said that the pupil-teacher's is a selected life which can well bear extra strain, since the medical certificate required at the outset sufficiently guards against his liability to injury under the stress of his duties. But facts seem to show that the medical certificate is worse than waste paper, or else that even the sound and strong are broken by the weight of the burden imposed. The testimony to the miserable physique induced by the pupil-teacher's life is melancholy to the last degree. Their very stature seems to be affected. " Almost always short of stature and pale-faced," says Mr. George Smith, " with the anxious, wearied look occasionally that young people ought never to wear." " Of rather diminutive stature and delicate health," says a quondam teacher, now a clergyman. " They grow or rather half-grow narrow-chested," says another, " flabby-muscled, round-shouldered, thin; their faces carry a care-worn, dreary expression." A lady teacher testifies, " They are very generally pale and delicate in appearance, with a droop in the shoulders and an anxious careworn expression in their faces while in repose. Their brain power can never be properly developed while they work to the extreme of their strength during the day." Another mistress: " In many cases their growth appears much stunted." · " A tall pupil teacher is almost a phenomenon in my experience," says an East-end mistress. " The body is sacrificed to the brain," writes a teacher from Kentish Town, " and both suffer in consequence." A lady now removed to the super-intendence of a well-known endowed middle-class school observes that " the *moral* strain in endeavouring to govern a class of 20, 30, or 40 children is excessively bad for growing youths and girls." Such testimonies as these might easily be multiplied without limit. Very striking is the remark of the head-mistress of one of the training colleges: " We have done a hard term's work, but these girls all look in better condition than when we received them from their pupil-teacher life."

Grave enough assuredly are these facts regarded solely in reference to the condition of an honourable and indispensable profession ; but contemplated from the point of view of our four million scholars,* they acquire a portentous significance. If, as I am persuaded, 50 per cent. of our whole teaching staff are overstrained by their labours or their anxieties, how fatal a flaw must this prove in their influence on the boys and girls submitted to their charge. Negatively, the listlessness and weariness of the teacher must inevitably rob the lessons he superintends of life and interest ; positively, the nervous irritability to which so many teachers pathetically confess, must fill the child's mind with vexation or fear in place of the sunny temper in which alone juvenile study can be healthfully or profitably pursued. But the stress of the demands made upon the childish brain itself renders the school-life to multitudes one long, painful, and pernicious strain, quite independently of the depressing lassitude or the hasty temper of the over-wrought masters, mistresses, and pupil-teachers.

To begin with, many schools call upon their scholars for an appalling amount of home-work. Two-and-a-half hours each evening is no uncommon thing. Boys hardly out of the infant school will sit with flushed and throbbing brow over book and slate till ten and even eleven at night. "The continuous occupation of the child-life," writes a very able and earnest teacher, "robs it of due recreation, and tends to destroy all *faculty*, although it may increase *capacity*." But more predominant now than excessive home-lessons is excessive over-time in school. Every school is compelled to exhibit a time-table, and that time-table must be approved by Her Majesty's Inspector. But the table is often little better than a fraud : the anxious teacher expands the five or five-and-a-half hours per diem which it exhibits to six or seven, or more. The quick children may escape these extra hours ; the dull and the delicate are prisoners without reprieve. They must be worked up to "passing" point, and this is the only way to do it. Schools are quoted which

* There were in 1881 on the English and Welsh registers 4,045,362 children. The average attendance for the whole of Great Britain was 3,848,011.

even hold three sessions in the day and another on the Saturday. How does all this affect the health of the scholars themselves?

The most common symptom of its injurious consequence is the talking of lessons in sleep, to which a chorus of inspectors, teachers, and parents bear united witness. "Dozens of instances," says Mr. Quayle, of Liverpool, head-master of St. Thomas' and St. Matthew's, "of complaints from parents concerning their children's loss of appetite, talking in sleep, languor, nervous state, indifference to childish sports, &c. No robustness or energy." Mr. John Steedman, of Nottingham, says that in his former school, where much hard work was done continuously, and where the population was settled, the regular boys were very small. He has been struck with the rapid growth of many of them during the year or two *after leaving school.* "The children would be better," writes a mistress, "both in mind and body, if their school-life was happier; the strain of the Code prevents this." "The children's health is placed, unfortunately," writes a master, "in competition with the schoolmaster's means of living." Anecdotes abound of parents visiting the school to remonstrate against the pressure put on their little ones, and vainly interceding for the remission of excessive lessons. "About a week ago," said a Lancashire mother the other day, "they began to cram my little one, and she not seven years old, for the examination. It was lessons morning, afternoon, and night, and you never saw her without her books. I don't understand all this learning, but at last I saw that they were killing her. So I went to the school and said that I could not let her work so hard. But they would not let her stop. They said she would do grandly. But I wanted to keep my child. So at last, with no end of difficulty, I got a medical certificate, and now I mean to keep her at home till the inspector's been and gone, I do." In Nottingham, not long since, the parents of a little girl, seeing her overdone and talking of lessons in her sleep, gave notice that they should keep her from school for a time. The teacher promptly called and offered a present if the child attended regularly! A mistress in Yorkshire was called before a Committee of her Board a few weeks since for unmercifully beating a girl eight years old on the head, because she failed to work a problem in arithmetic (Standard III.). When the mother complained, the answer was that the child was clever enough and could do the sum if she chose. The parents pleaded that she was delicate, and that they would much rather she did not pass the examination till the next year if any severity had to be used. To which answered the teacher : " But I *want my money*, and I'll *make* her pass." That teacher put the whole system of "payment by results " in a nutshell.

We must not dismiss this branch of our inquiry without noting the effect of the requirements on *eyesight*—especially of the needle-work on the eyesight of girls. It is well known that alarm has arisen on this subject in Germany, and that many persons tax the minutely differentiated German printed character with much of the mischief. But like results accrue in England with no such type to bear the blame. A Birmingham mistress writes : "A very large proportion of my scholars suffer from diseases of the eye. Girls are frequently absent for weeks together attending the eye infirmaries. One pupil-teacher became temporarily blind while attempting to complete the needle-work for an examination." Another mistress, in whose school failing eyesight is very common, says, " the sewing (required under the New Code) is something terrible." " Sight," says a third mistress, " is a rapidly increasing failing among the scholars." A few years ago, H. M. Inspector, in a midland town, having conscientiously appraised the needlework of the elder infants grouped before him, turned to the mistress and asked, " Now can you show me any *pinafores by the three-year olds ?* " " No, indeed, sir," said she, taking the question for a solemn joke. " Oh, but I assure you *I get them in other schools,*" rejoined the official incarnation of the educational ideal of English statesmanship.

In her address to the Elementary Teachers' Union, at Sheffield, on " Over-Pressure in Schools," Miss Müller said :

" To any one watching the progress of a school, be it boys', girls', or infants', which attains annual good 'results,' the signs of over-pressure will be visible, though not to the passing visitor, who exclaims in astonishment at the rows of class-rooms abnormally clean, and the rows of children abnormally quiet. A superficial glance at any large institution discovers only appearances, and not realities. But let any one follow the course of such a school during a year or two with quiet and constant visits, and he will see little signs that have large meanings. There are certain evidences which are unmistakable. The visitor will ask himself, ' Do the children look happy?' Alas, never! ' Do the teachers look happy?' Still less."* Mr. Sykes, the late President of the Teachers' Union, speaks with authority, at any rate on the views of teachers. " To a dull child," says he, " our present system of cram and mechanical drill must make the schoolroom appear as a place of cruel mental torture. . . . Babies, of four or five years of age, are subjected to [the mania for competitive examination]; and children of seven years of age earn grants upon their ability to satisfy the inspector, after passing through the ordeal of individual examination. The pale faces, lack-lustre eyes, aching brains of the little children, and the repeated complaints of brain-fever, loss of eye-sight, and bodily depression and weakness, plainly evince the cruelty as well as the senselessness of the system." † As to the " babies of four or five years of age," an ingenuous inspector laments, in his report, that " a very useful year of school-life is frequently lost because the attendance officer can ask no questions about a child under five." ‡ I have a curly-locked, bright-eyed baby of just that age; I am glad he is not " useful " in earning grants for anybody!

An infallible index to the *general* depression of the health of the children in our Elementary Schools is to be found in the *exceptional* and permanent break-downs, and even deaths from over-pressure, testified to from so many quarters.

* Report of the N.U.E.T., 1882, p. lxxviii.
† *Ibid*, pp. xxix., xxviii.   ‡ Report of the C. C. E., 1881—2, p. 418.

These cases are difficult to get at, owing to the natural reticence of those who know; still more difficult to prove, because the *post hoc* is not necessarily the *propter hoc*. Still, it is impossible to doubt their frequent occurrence. "Two cases," writes one head-master, "are conspicuous in my mind." "Some two years ago," says a Liverpool master, "a very intelligent, but delicate boy entered the school, anxious to compete for one of the scholarships established by the Liverpool Council of Education. After being in the school less than six months he died, the immediate cause of death being rheumatism of the heart; but during the delirium of the last few days, he moaned sadly about his school-work." "My medical adviser," a teacher writes to me from Bristol, "asserts that brain-fever is frequently the result of home-pressure, and that the number of such cases has been on the increase for some years." A lady in the service of the Board at Birmingham, writes: "To maintain a percentage in upper classes meeting Code requirements, I have had to raise a good number from Standard II. to Standard IV. The parents of one child whom I had put forward objected strongly, on the ground that 'last year but one,' said the mother, 'my other girl was served the same, and the very week after the examination she was taken ill and died.' Of course," adds the teacher, "I respected the mother's wishes, but I was not able to set aside the principle; some other Standard II. child—the next best I could find—had to fill her place." A Bradford master writes to me: "I have heard of many instances in the town of permanent break-down or death resulting from the strain of school-work. A few years ago a girl committed suicide owing to depression of spirits caused by her inability to do the home-work prescribed at school." Mr. Girling, at a recent meeting of the executive of the National Union of Elementary Teachers, referred to the case of a child who had then just died of brain-fever, whose continual cry in his last delirium was, "I can't get it right! I can't get it right!" At the last annual meeting of the Scotch Educational Institute, Dr. Farquharson said that lassitude, depression, and dyspepsia had frequently come under his observation among the Common School children, and especially chorea, or St. Vitus's dance, and he added that the grimaces and eccentric movements of incipient chorea were sometimes chastised as pieces of impudent buffoonery. At the same congress, Dr. Robert Beveridge; Physician to the Aberdeen Royal Infirmary, gave statistics of the increase of deaths from diseases of the brain among children of school age in the eight large towns of Scotland in the decade 1872—81, when the Education Act was in force, as compared with 1859—68. Dr. Beveridge has been kind enough to assist me in reducing these statistics to exact tabular form. He compares first the percentage of deaths during school age by brain disease with deaths from all causes for the two periods, and then the percentage of deaths by brain disease with deaths from all causes except zymotics, which are, of course, very irregular. This is the result :— *

	Percentage of Deaths from Diseases of the Brain to Deaths from all Causes during School-age.		Percentage of Deaths from Diseases of the Brain to Deaths from all Causes, except Zymotic Diseases, during School-age.	
	1859—1868.	1872—1881.	1859—1868.	1872—1881.
Aberdeen	7·5	9·2	11·3	12·7
Dundee	5	8·4	8·4	12·2
Edinburgh	6·6	7·7	10·27	13·4
Glasgow....................	5·5	7·3	8·4	9·9
The eight large towns of Scotland	5·8	7·7	9·05	10·95

Enough has, perhaps, now been said to establish the

* These figures, covering about a third of the population of Scotland, and comparing whole decades, are on a large enough scale to exclude casual sources of fallacy. Their significance will, perhaps, be more apparent when converted into the following form :—

	Increase of proportion of deaths from Brain Disease to deaths from all sources. Per cent.			Increase of proportion of deaths from Brain Disease to deaths from all sources except zymotics. Per cent.
Aberdeen	22·67	...	...	12·39
Dundee	68	...	...	45·24
Edinburgh	16·67	...	...	30·48
Glasgow	32·73	...	...	17·86
The Eight large Towns of Scotland... ...	32·76	...	...	20·99

Dr. Beveridge has extracted his figures from the returns of the Registrar-

fact that there is among teachers and children in our Elementary Schools (1) a widespread depression of health, and (2) too high a percentage of complete physical or mental collapses. But it must not be supposed that this state of things is attributable *solely* to the high-pressure system which is so much to be deplored. The evil effects of bad methods of work are redoubled by bad sanitary arrangements.

The principal requirements of the Education Department, from a sanitary point of view, are that 80 cubic feet of internal space and eight square feet of internal area shall be allowed in every school-building for each unit of average attendance; and that managers shall not fail, after six months' notice, to remedy any such defect in the premises as seriously interferes with the efficiency of the school. Failure here may, under the New Code, incur the loss of half the whole grant earned. The Department further

General, the only source available. In these returns ages are arranged in four classes:—(1) Under 5 years; (2) 5 to 20; (3) 20 to 60; and (4) over 60 years. Hence Dr. Beveridge is compelled to take school age as 5—20 years without further sub-division. The large proportion of the Scotch town population going on to the High Schools and the Universities renders this prolonged schoolage less vitiating for our purpose than it would be for English lives; but undoubtedly the pressure in these advanced seminaries, which is notorious, constitutes an appreciable factor in our results. The *chief* disease of the brain or nervous system among persons between 5 and 20 is cephalitis, or inflammation of the brain proper. Death from convulsions, which would otherwise be a highly vitiating element, not depending on such causes as we are investigating, is almost entirely confined to infants under 5 years. Dr. Beveridge has kindly supplied me with these figures for the eight large towns of Scotland (1881), which will show the proportion in which different nervous disorders prove fatal at different ages:—

	Age: 0—5	5—20	20—60	60—	Total.
Cephalitis	350	110	47	8	515
Apoplexy	86	34	280	296	696
Paralysis...	11	11	221	440	683
Insanity ...	0	0	10	6	16
Chorea ...	0	2	1	0	3
Epilepsy ...	9	11	44	14	78
Convulsions	453	31	12	2	498
Diseases of Brain in other forms or undefined ...	60	68	164	90	382
Total ...	969	267	779	856	2,871

requires generally to be satisfied that the premises are healthy, well lighted, warmed, drained, and ventilated.

Such provision proves in the working miserably inefficient for its ends. The close, stuffy atmosphere of nine school-rooms out of ten after an hour's occupation is truly horrible. Indeed, how could it possibly be otherwise? Eighty cubic feet per child, says the English Department: Professor Pettenkofer, of Munich, lends his high authority to a demand for 540 cubic feet per child. We put twenty-seven children into the class-room which he declares is only fit for four! In a hundred ways premises passed without a criticism by H. M. Inspectors are disqualified for the child's abiding place during one-fourth part of its existence. Light falling in the wrong direction, knife-board seats, seats so high that the poor little feet dangle, all these blemishes leave the grant untouched. Miss Löfving tells us how in the schools of the London Board, the child's left arm is placed on the desk above the copy-book or slate, the trunk twisted and bent to the left, the left side of the chest and abdomen pressing with full weight against the desk—a posture disastrous to growth, to respiration, to circulation, to digestion, and to spinal development. "When remonstrating," says she, "against this barbarity, I got the astonishing answer, that this position was enjoined by *the Government Inspector, 'in order to prevent the children copying from each other.'"* *

We have then to face the fact of terrible physical evil in our national system of education—a wholesale undermining of health which must tell with redoubled power in the second generation. Now, I believe the unexpressed feeling of many excellent people might be summed up thus: No doubt it is a very sad thing that some should be struck down and many maimed, but after all it is worth great sacrifices to become an educated nation; if the minority suffer, yet the majority have great gain; and we must not look only at the victims of the battle, but also at the splendid fruits of victory. It becomes necessary then to ask, *Are* we becom-

* *Lecture on Physical Education and its place in a Rational System of Education.* By Concordia Löfving, p. 44.

ing an educated nation ? What is the calibre of the education bestowed at so great a cost ?

Teachers, at any rate, are almost unanimous that to two classes of children a good education—an education good *for them*—is by the present system absolutely denied. First, the clever children are defrauded of the proper fruits of their talent, for they are dragged back by the dullards and the dunces. The interested teacher has no interest in leading them forward apace : the disinterested teacher has no time to spare to them from the backward. Secondly, the dull children are forced in a manner that robs them of what little brain-power they begin with. They must be presented in a higher standard each successive year, and if possible by any pulling or pushing, they must be passed. To the average child, a good many authorities agree, the requirements of the Code are pretty fairly adjusted. Now by a trick of thought, it is common to assume that the average children are the majority, that non-average children are the exception. But in reality there are very few average children indeed ; and if first we subtract those for whom the Code moves too slowly, and next those for whom it goes too fast, we shall have a very meagre class left to benefit by its measured scale of progress. The truth, however, would appear to be that its pitch is that of the *rather* clever children ; so that on the one side the few *very* clever children suffer by its leniency, and on the other the combined mass of the average children and the slow suffer by its stringency.

It is the *driving*, then, which is the major evil in the educational working of the Code. A horse spurred up a steep hill will stop dead beat before it gains the top. " It is a common thing," writes a Birmingham teacher, " for children who have been driven through the lower standards, when reaching the fourth to fail utterly, and leave school with an utter distaste for study." " The fundamental work of the ' three R's ' is not half as well done as it was twenty years ago," says another ; " boys who begin bright get quite stupid by the time they are in Standard IV." Mr. Quayle says, " Children just scrape through an examination, and are then placed (per Code) in a higher standard, where the work is far beyond their comprehension. To ensure a pass, they are then forced, goaded, and crammed, till work is made hateful to them, and their intellect is dulled. This goes on year after year till they get exemption from attendance at school, when books are cast aside and the groundwork so laborously prepared, is seldom made use of." Mr. John Reynolds, headmaster of the splendid school at Flowery Field, near Manchester, and on the whole the warmest friend of the Codes Old and New I have met with among teachers, alleges that " where an attempt is made to get extraordinary percentages, dunces are worried into deeper stolidity." Mr. Francombe, of the Redcliffe Endowed Boys' School, at Bristol, allows me to quote his opinion that " the number of subjects now being taught in our schools greatly impairs the results in the 'three R's,' and that *but few boys leave our schools able to write well and spell correctly.*" A colleague in the same city corroborates : " Nothing is learnt really well, only a smattering of each subject being taught to each child, as the requirements are too many to be mastered in the time." Mr. Hodgson, of Kidderminster, complains that " there is not time to train children to think." This view is more strongly put by a lady now freed from the trammels and conducting with the highest success a school that knows neither Code nor Standard. She holds that the " payment by results " system " is admirably calculated to further mechanical cram and trickery and discourage all true educators with noble aims." " What will pass, not what will educate, is the incentive," says Mr. George Smith. Mr. Steedman has placed in my hands a most careful paper on the whole question. While not deeming the Code requirements as in themselves excessive, he holds that it is only suitable for children " not harassed by multifarious work or home-duties which occupy the mind with other subjects and hinder *that process of germination* which ought to ensue between positive study and study."

It is worth while to observe in what manner the system strikes at thoughtful teaching and induces "cram." A female teacher whom I have already quoted, after sighing over the process by which " the dunces are with pain untold brought to ' passing' pitch," says, "I once heard a Second Standard examined in geography. There were ten out of the thirty whose knowledge of Physical Geography might have put grown people to the blush, and the rest acquitted themselves not dishonourably. Yet, in the report, the teacher's only reward was, ' The answering in Standard II. should be more general.' How think you the teacher prepared her class for the next examination? By the *rule of grind;* so many through the mill : and the report this time *gave her great praise.*" I have been furnished with a kindred illustration from another branch: " Mr. L——, head master of St. —— School, felt very dissatisfied with the results of his arithmetical teaching, although his school passed very creditable examinations. The whole work seemed to him too mechanical, and consequently little helpful in developing the intelligence of his scholars. He changed his methods. He taught next on first principles. He was delighted to see the ingenuity shown by the children in inventing processes. The answers certainly were not always correct, but that was owing to mechanical drill having given place to rational methods, which might be a little less reliable for answers, but which were more fruitful of thought-life. The well-known book of Sonnenschein and Nesbitt was his *vade mecum.* The examination came round at last. If the ' intelligence' of his school should be now tested he was sanguine. But intelligence could not be tested by a dumb card with one or two arithmetical puzzles on it. The ' results' of the examination were bad. The grant was poor. Next year Mr. L—— turned Sonnenschein out, and returned to the old and profitable plan, getting a good grant for his reward."

And if teachers speak thus hopelessly of their own work, what have Inspectors to say? Truly I believe some of them know but little of it; yet many clearly see its failings.

"Year after year," writes Mr. Brodie, "the same complaints are in every Inspector's report. The teaching is dry, bookish, technical, barren." Yet this same Inspector boldly defends the test by percentages of passes. "They attest," he declares, "when high, to at least much solid hard work, dogged labour, and persistent every-day drudgery." Alas! they do. But doggedness and drudgery, these will make neither bright nor intelligent children. Mr. Barrington-Ward confides to "my lords" his experiences thus: "Too many elementary teachers, men and women alike, still fancy that it is sufficient to aim at mere mechanical excellence, to the exclusion of the development of those rational faculties which raise man to his noble rank above the brute creation. With some teachers whom I could name a parrot or a monkey would almost form as apt a pupil as his present charges." This is very impressive writing, though not quite grammatical; but Mr. Barrington-Ward should remember that for twenty years our teachers have been assiduously taught that if they diverge from mechanical teaching the average wage of forty shillings a week is likely to drop to thirty-five. Mr. Alderson, one of the best and kindest of Inspectors (though I grieve to find him going for increase of school hours), finds little benefit to true education from the multitude of "subjects," in addition to the "three R's," which throng the modern Codes. He finds in too many of the schools of busy Marylebone "Reading, which does not expand the mind; grammar, which does not leaven speech and writing; arithmetic, which does not form a habit of exact thinking; geography, which does not interest the imagination; literature, that does not improve the taste; physiology, that has no bearing on the simple laws of health; domestic economy, that does not contribute to the comfort of homes."

No, we are not yet becoming "an educated nation."

I shall be met with the rejoinder that I have failed to recognise the amendment in all this negative and positive evil likely to result from the introduction of Mr. Mundella's New Code. Teachers are almost unanimous in acknowledging the high-minded desire to do good which has actuated Mr. Mundella in the preparation of this now famous document, and the gracious courtesy and kindness with which, in bright contrast to some of his predecessors, he has striven to comprehend and to meet their views; an acknowledgment most thoroughly deserved. But unhappily teachers are almost equally unanimous in the apprehension that the New Code will prove very nearly as oppressive as any of its predecessors, if not even more so.*

That Code retains the principle, but modifies the method, of " payment by results." In Infant Schools the total possible grant is to be seventeen shillings per unit of average attendance. Of this, nine shillings is fixed and depends in no way on results. Two, four, or six shillings may be awarded as the " merit grant," of which more anon. Two shillings will depend on results in needlework and singing. In Boys' Schools, the highest possible (excluding grants on " special subjects ") will be £1 0s. 10d. per unit of average attendance—viz., four shillings and sixpence fixed independently of results; one, two, or three shillings, merit grant; eight shillings and fourpence, depending on an exact percentage test; and five shillings, depending on a rough percentage test.† In Girls' Schools one shilling extra is possible, viz., the grant for needlework. In addition to these amounts, however, individual scholars may be presented for examination in one or in two " specific subjects," and for each individual pass under this head, the grant will be swelled by four shillings. The merit grant is an entirely new element in the Government allowance. It is undoubtedly conceived in the true interests of education, and

* Inspectors seem to expect that the New Code will either leave things pretty much as they are or increase the pressure all round. Mr. Collins, Inspector for the Peterborough district : " With regard to the New Code, generally, he might say that the examinations would, as far as possible, go on the same lines as in past years."—(*Schoolmaster,* Feb. 3, 1883.) Mr. Hitchens, Inspector for the Huddersfield district: " No doubt it gave them all more work."—(*Schoolmaster,* Feb. 17, 1883.)

† The " Instructions to Inspectors " suggests 75 per cent. in " class subjects " for " good," which is understood to earn the full grant, 50 per cent. for " fair," which will earn the half grant under this last head.

nothing can be more admirable than the description given by " my lords " of the " excellent " school entitled to the highest award under this head.* But the Inspector is still instructed to regard " the number of passes "—in other words the percentage—as an important element in the award of the merit grant ; and quantity being so much easier to assess than quality, there is every reason to fear that this will form, in the majority of districts, the real foundation on which merit will be calculated, quality, and, still more, general organisation and tone, being more or less shadowy accessories in the inspector's mind. Indeed, though " the rage for percentages " which teacher after teacher has deplored, may be in some degree checked by the New Code, the temptation to the teacher to wring the utmost possible quantitative results out of the brains of the largest number possible of children will be as stringent under the New Code as the Old ; nor will it make much difference in the stress of that temptation whether the teacher's pittance is to be directly measured by the results obtained or whether he is only working in the fear of managers whose pride and (in Voluntary Schools) whose pockets will be affected by the rise or the fall in grant. No child whose name has been on the register within the last twenty-two weeks, it must be remembered, may be withheld from examination without the express and individual sanction of the Inspector ; every child must be presented in a standard higher than that in which he was presented the year before, unless the Inspector give express and individual permission to the contrary, and the First Standard must be taken at seven years old. The loud and unanimous appeal of the teachers all over the land is to be allowed to withhold from examination at least one child in ten on their own responsibility, and to be entrusted on their own responsibility with greater freedom of classification according to the ability—as distinguished from the age—of their pupils.

The concession of this dual demand would, no doubt, miti-

* " Instructions to Inspectors," Sec. 32.

gate the monstrous evils of the unhappy system that is in vogue; but I am persuaded that while the broad principle of " payment by results " continues in the ascendant, over-pressure, rule of thumb, and the perversion of the true ends of education will prevail over the length and breadth of the land. Let teachers rather look to the New Ministerial Circular of Upper Canada, where, in the upper grades at least, a clean sweep is made of payment by result. Let them ask, with one of my own correspondents, " If the teachers in Germany and America can be trusted to do their work without being required to make all children pass a certain examination each year, why may not we ? " As it is, our allies in the methods of education on all the face of the globe are, in some respects, it would appear, Austria and China only !

But it is not the method only, but the aim as well, that is in fault, not the practice alone, but the ideal too. Two supreme mistakes vitiate the whole organisation of English education, from the Elementary Schools, through the Grammar Schools and Girls' High Schools, to the Universities. The first mistake is the conception of intellectual training as the acquisition of information rather than the development of faculty. The second mistake is the conception of intellectual training as itself constituting education, whereas education is the co-ordinate and inter-dependent development of physical, intellectual, and moral faculty.

Of the first mistake this only need be said : it springs out of the trading spirit in which education is regarded, the trading spirit which was the inspiration of Mr. Lowe, and corroded all his work ; yet even from the purely commercial point of view it is utterly fallacious. Not the boy stuffed with " crammed " facts (even if he did not disgorge them the moment schooling ends) makes the good clerk or the successful merchant, but the boy of thoughtful energy. Many a rich man of to-day never went to school at all after six years old. Well spoke a thriving Glasgow shoemaker a month or two ago : " Education Act a success? Why, before the Act my apprentices used to come to me unable to read or write, but they'd rise to an idea like a trout to a fly. Now they all write well enough, but they've no brightness or intelligence."

But the second mistake is the fatal one—the conception of intellectual education as something which machinery may produce apart from the development of the other faculties of our humanity. I will not speak now of moral training. The Inspector is, indeed, instructed to satisfy himself " that all reasonable care is taken, in the ordinary management of the school, to bring up the children in the habits of punctuality, of good manners and language, of cleanliness and neatness, and also to impress upon the children the importance of cheerful obedience to duty, of consideration and respect for others, and of honour and truthfulness in word and act." * If the conditions of inspection and examination were not directly inimical to some of these requirements, a higher value might be set upon this paragraph than, as it is, is possible. It is perhaps useless here to express the grief and shame that arise from the reflection that the chaotic condition of religious opinion compels the unnatural divorce of religious from intellectual training in the common schools of the country—an arrangement which not only emaciates the intellectual education itself, but fosters the pernicious conception of religion as a thing apart from the daily concerns of life. And this is said with the full knowledge that no amendment is possible till the nation is baptized with a new faith, and the vivid sense of religious realities penetrates the national thought and life.

The failure of educationists in this country, however, to recognise the need of interpenetrating intellectual with physical education, must be discussed at greater length. Parliament and the Department have charged themselves with certain responsibilities in regard to the physical welfare of the child. However ineffectually they discharge it, they freely acknowledge the duty of guarding the scholar from overt physical injury. Negatively they hold them-

* Cited from the Code of 1881, in " Instructions to Inspectors," Sec. 32.*

selves responsible. They have failed to perceive that, if they undertake to educate, they have to take in charge positive physical development. It is not enough to say, "We will guard this child from bad air and bad smells." It would not be enough even to *do* it, as well as to say it. If you are going to educate, you must educate body as well as mind; indeed, you cannot truly do the one without the other. Speaking of the mass, not of the exceptional individual, it is certain that you cannot have sound minds, save by securing sound bodies as their instruments. If you try for the former, neglecting the latter, the mind will fail of true health; and every effort to develop it alone will react with fearful force upon the body. "Overstrain in Education" will not stop when adequate ventilation is secured and hours of mental toil are limited; it will go on till physical development is sought by positive agencies as careful and elaborate as those designed for the promotion of intellectual progress.

"The art of education" writes (of all men) Professor Bain, "assumes a certain average of physical health, and does not inquire into the means of keeping up or increasing that average." Alas! that is so in Great Britain; but so it ought not to be. True education is the harmonious development of all the powers towards the perfect man. It is not the traders only of the future that fill our schools, but the citizens and parents. Mr. Colt-Williams fears for our future army and navy if the present school curriculum is extended. But physical vigour is no less needful to the sound citizenship of the civilian; and in the light of our modern knowledge of heredity, terrible indeed is the responsibility resting on any legislators who strain the physique of the fathers and mothers that are to be.

Just as much, then, as it is the duty of the State to strive to develop a higher intelligence in the rising generation, is it incumbent upon it to take measures as an essential element in national education for the development of a higher healthiness. Having once laid its constraining hand upon our boys and girls, it must either make or mar, physically no less than intellectually : and it is bound not to mar, but make.

If this grave national obligation once be recognised, many hours of the present brain-labour will have to be swept away to make room for the physical culture which alone can secure sound results even in the intellectual sphere. The games of our little ones will be seen to be no less important than their lessons ; the play-ground will be as essential as the school-room. The " run out " at the end of every hour, while doors and windows are flung open to let the air sweep through, will be a part of the school discipline. Hygienic seats and desks will be universally required. And all this blessed reformation will be consummated by a complete, graduated, scientific course of gymnastic education—not the weekly drill based on the requirements of military evolution and superintended by a pompous sergeant dressed in a little brief authority, but the daily exercise of all the muscles of the body based on physiological laws.

The gratitude of all educational reformers and all be-lievers in the high functions of humanity, is due to Miss Löfving for her efforts, in succession to Dr. Roth, to inspire English educators with a sense of the high sanctity of their calling and the miserable failure of their practice. Espe-cially is it to be hoped that she may succeed in awakening interest in the gymnastic system elaborated by her celebrated countryman and predecessor, Ling. The London School Board has actually listened to her pleadings, and allowed her to exhibit the Swedish methods. But when she went so far as to ask for three half-hours in the week for the girls of London to practise the Ling gymnastics, " payment by results " forbade it ; and these children—many of them without any true physical exercise whatever—must content themselves with fulfilling Mr. Brodie's ideal, " solid hard work, dogged labour, and persistent every-day drudgery," to the end of the chapter.*

---

* It was my intention, when I undertook this article, not to confine the discussion to the " Overstrain " in Primary Schools, but to adduce evidence of its widespread existence in the middle and higher classes ; and I am

With all the splendid progress which has marked our century, with all the battles won against ignorance, and indebted to several head-mistresses and others connected with the education now offered in Girls' High Schools for furnishing me with the fruits of their experience and the expression of their views. But I have found it impossible, in the present paper, to go beyond the limits of the narrower subject treated in the text. The rapid spread, however, of Girls' High Schools throughout the country, superseding by their cheapness many excellent private seminaries, makes the nature of the education given in them and the attention accorded to physical considerations, a question of more than private interest and importance. The Girls' Public Day-School Company now possesses twenty-seven establishments in different parts of the country, with 4,800 pupils, and there are a growing number of schools modelled more or less on the pattern of these, under local committees of gentlemen and ladies. The Company aspires to set the tone of education for middle-class girls. It is a pleasure to be allowed to quote Miss Hastings, head mistress of the Wimbledon High School, to the effect that the Company are "most wise and thoughtful" in refraining from pressing the responsible teachers for educational results which the mistresses think excessive; but I fear they do not always exercise over mistresses who adopt other views and methods of education than Miss Hastings, such a supervision as shall check the excessive stimulus of which there is such frequent complaint. Miss Hastings declines to send in any of her pupils for outside examinations, such as the Oxford and Cambridge "Locals;" but in other schools, both within and outside the control of the Company, the utmost stress is laid upon these examinations as tests of work done, and a distinguished head-mistress, though not prepared to set her face against them, still writes to me that, in her opinion, the Council are misled at times in the direction of too strongly urging examinations by the success of schools which purchase their distinction at the heavy price of overwork. Under mistresses such as I have quoted, the health of the scholars is all that can be desired; but of those schools where the lady principals stimulate the ambition of their pupils, or fail to check the eagerness of those whose natural ambition is excessive, a very different story must be told. "During the examination week," writes an assistant teacher, "I have known of several girls going into hysterics, who are not usually at all wanting in self-control; and I have known of two fainting in the midst of an examination." "Girls are so anxious," says another lady of much experience in High Schools, though not, I believe, under the Company, "that they work themselves up to almost a frenzy of excitement from nervous dread of failure." Yet the Principal of one of the Company's schools writes to me :—" I have known cases in which excitable girls, instead of being rather checked, have been urged on by constant inquiries by their parents about marks, &c., first to get to the top of their respective forms, and then to pass various outside examinations, till their nervous systems have been completely overdone." And though this lady lays the chief blame on the parents, who urge their daughters on, yet, on the one hand, certainly many parents are constantly protesting against the school demands, and, on the other, it is the school system that is responsible for suggesting to parents

filth, and vice, in grasp of what is meant by the training of a human being, we have fallen behind the fellow-
these mad and criminal ambitions. " Girls," says the same lady,
"who are pressed on at the early age of the Junior Cambridge to take
high honours often break down completely, and do no more. So also with
the Senior. I hear grievous complaints from Newnham and Girton that
the girls from certain schools have been so overworked before coming up
that they can do nothing at Cambridge." An assistant teacher writes to
me :—" In High Schools it depends entirely on the head mistress of each
school whether there is overwork or not." She adds her opinion—after an
experience in three High Schools—that " all marks, positions, prizes, &c.,
ought to be done away with, and the pupils should work for the sake of
the good they get from the work. It is not the work, but the anxiety
and strain that accompanies the work which does the harm. Girls sometimes get a mark-fever, never satisfied unless they get the highest mark.
I see them rush for corrected papers with flushed faces and trembling
hands, look at the end for the mark, and then stuff them into their desks.
It is not the work they care about, but what they get for the work," which
reminds me of a youth who afterwards took the Balliol, at Oxford, in an
exceptionally brilliant examination. When I knew him he was the most
wonderful prize-getter—no matter in what subject—I ever fell in with.
His true culture was indicated by the fact that his college room was
adorned with tawdry and vulgar coloured prints, and he always emphati
cally protested that he cared not at all for knowledge, nor for distinction,
but only for the *money value of his winnings*. I will conclude this note by
transcribing the major part of an admirable letter from the mistress of a
non-Company High School in the North of England. She writes :—

" There are few subjects upon which I feel so strongly as that of physical
education and development ; especially as it seems to take such a very
secondary place in many public girls' schools, and is frequently altogether
neglected.

"1. I think one of the greatest evils is the local examinations for girls
under eighteen years of age. They put a great strain upon them. The
girls unconsciously get over-excited, and where the examination is constantly held before them as the goal to which they are tending, they
think more of it than the work they are actually doing. Young children,
especially, if they are not stupid and apathetic, become unnaturally
excited. Work might possibly be arranged in a school so that the girls
were unconscious of an approaching examination in it, but this is very
difficult to accomplish with such as the Oxford and Cambridge Local
Examinations. In my opinion it is better in Girls' High Schools to arrange
for a systematic course of education suited to the ages, capacity, and to a
certain extent local characteristics of the girls, and subject the school
periodically to an inspection. This does away with prolonged strain and
enables thorough work to be tested. The Oxford and Cambridge Local
Examinations require a knowledge of a great many subjects, and young
children should not be occupied with more than a very few at one time
For this last reason I consider them very injurious. Again, failure is often
taken very much to heart, especially by the best, most thoughtful, intelli-

citizens of Pericles and the sophists with whom Socrates held dispute.   They at least knew that the whole man

gent and conscientious girls, and it is they who as a rule do not succeed well in examinations. The result is that they are disappointed; they lose confidence in themselves, and become indifferent. Their intelligence gets blunted, and all spirit for investigation and research is crushed out by the thought that there is no time for anything but that which is needed for the examination. I think the very feeling of having accomplished some thing intellectually adds to bodily vigour and energy, and then follows the desire for exercise. I have seen girls after thinking out some question, and finally arriving at a right conclusion, being seized with the desire to rush about and play. But this healthy feeling never comes to a girl who is crammed.

"2. No school should be without a spacious playground and a large, airy room for wet weather. The system of turning girls out for ten or even five minutes in the middle of the morning for an orderly march round a corridor or playground, is, in my opinion, altogether unnatural. So is supervision by a teacher during play, unless she plays with them at their request. A large number of girls together will generally play, and play well and heartily, if left to themselves for fifteen minutes, and not need supervision.

"3. A portion of every day should be given to systematic drill. For older girls of 17 and 18, gymnastics might be substituted for drill, or supplement it with advantage. A good school should have its gymnasium and, if possible, swimming bath.

"4. I think that, as a rule, far too much written work is expected from girls. The bent, cramped position over a desk, for a length of time, is bad for them, both at school and at home. It increases the duties of the teachers enormously, for all written work should be carefully looked over and corrected. Children would be brighter, and their knowledge would be more thorough, for more 'question and answer' in class; and the time thus spent in catechising would, although apparently taken from the lesson, be spent to the greater advantage of the pupils.

"5. If girls are kept on the mental stretch for nearly four hours in the morning, that is, for two hours at a time, with an interval of half-an-hour in the middle for drill and play, very little good work can be expected from them in addition. In many High Schools girls work, I may say, literally always. They come home at one o'clock, begin to work immediately after dinner, take no walk or exercise, or, if they are forced to go out, think all the way of their lessons. They work again all the evening until late at night, perhaps until 11 o'clock, and even then they do not rest, but think of a Euclid rider or some other mathematical problem the last thing, and leave it to solve itself during the night by unconscious cerebration. In the morning it has to be hastily written out, and the girl leaves home without having time left to eat her breakfast. This is not education; and a school which allows such a state of things to continue must have something very much amiss with its organisation. Hard, bright class-work, with a little carefully-set work to do at home on the day's lesson, is in my opinion the best economy, and I have found it answer.

"6. If teachers are conscientiously to prepare their lessons, and I main-

must be trained if the parts were to be sound. Those schools of Athens, which bred the highest type of intellect which has ever adorned the human race, were all gymnasia. The young men, whose university was the Academy or the Lyceum, equipped themselves with immortal philosophy and mathematics while they walked among the orange-trees and myrtles; and health meant with them what the word means in its old Anglo-Saxon strength, wholeness of all the faculties which make up humanity.

In her essay on "Hygeiolatry," Miss Cobbe owns to the gravest apprehension lest modern society should be invaded by a new principle in morals. The threatening principle she reduces to this formula: "That any practice which, in the opinion of experts, conduces to health or tends to the cure of disease, becomes, *ipso facto*, morally lawful and right.* Nor is it easy to escape the facts which Miss Cobbe marshals to prove her case. Rightly or wrongly, legislation for health is carried forward with a zeal which takes but scanty heed of constitutional principles and personal rights for which our forefathers spent treasure of means and life. Rightly or wrongly, not only the warehouse and the mill, but the home and the actual person are more and more subjected to inspection and control which neither we nor our fathers have hitherto been able to bear.

But the strange thing is that side by side with this phenomenon, contemporaneously with the appearance of the degrading and deadly doctrine which Miss Cobbe deplores, and of the good and true spirit of sanitary reform which is the brighter side of the medal, we have a growing recklessness about healthy living, which makes for the

tain that the simplest lesson needs preparation, they must not be burdened with the drudgery of correcting endless exercises. A teacher in a High School should not have her time so filled up that she cannot correct all her exercise-books within school hours. This, however, is generally the case, owing probably to an inadequate staff. I do not believe a teacher in full work can at the same time take an examination herself satisfactorily. I have never known of a case of its being done without a breakdown sooner or later, or without some detriment to health."

* "The Peak in Darien," &c., p. 82.

serious deterioration of the stalwart English race. While health-committees of Town Councils are more vigilant than any previous generation has known them, barristers, solicitors, physicians, ministers of religion by the hundred are living at a pressure of which the lightest result is chronic dyspepsia and consequent enfeebled progeny, while among the graver consequents are heart-disease, consumption, paralysis, insanity, early death. While food-reform and dress-reform are becoming the social gospel of thousands of educated ladies, I for one have frequently reckoned up the whole circle of my personal acquaintances in the vain attempt to find a single unbroken family of vigorous and healthy girls. While local and national legislators freely sanction, in the interests of health, regulations which empower sanitary officers to enter the private house and carry off the sick child against the protest of the parent, the school which the State endows reeks with foul air, and the school-keeper is bribed to goad the slow brain till it keeps pace with the quick. While physiology and domestic economy are earning heavy grants from the State purse, the simplest physiological laws are ignored, and the first principles of sanitary economy are defied by the agents of State education.

The anomaly springs from one fundamental cause. The criminal excess and the criminal defect in the care for health equally arise from a great lack in our social and religious philosophy. That lack is an *ethics of the body*.

The only true ethics of the body consists in its recognition as an instrument for responsible use—a recognition which can be generated only by a vivid religious sense of its direct derivation from the Supreme in trust for the furtherance of the noblest purposes of life. Such a recognition will, on the one hand, check the disposition to regard physical sanitation as the ultimate end of the existence of the individual or the race. It will, on the other hand, constrain each man by its moral force towards thoughtful and steady solicitude for his own health and that of the community of which he is a responsible unit. Under the guidance of such a principle, we shall neither exalt the care of the body to be the final goal of our social aims, nor leave the body to shift for itself unconsidered and untended.

Guided by such an ethics, the citizen will perceive the avoidable over-taxing of his own physical powers and the indulgence of idle and selfish habits to be alike immoral. A voluntary spendthrift mental strain and a voluntary inactivity he will know to be equal sins; and he will no longer, while gravely telling his neighbour he does wrong to overwork, cherish a secret persuasion that his own overwork leans to the side of virtue. We shall all understand it to be our duty to maintain our physical constitutions at the highest level of efficiency we can, to the end that " our bodies may be the servants of our spirits, and both our bodies and our spirits be God's servants."

But if such is the obligation of the professional man in his own case, how far graver the obligation with regard to the young and tender minds and frames committed to his charge. Here are men not made, but men and women in the making. The delicate balance of physical, intellectual, and moral power can be sustained in the process of development only by the wisest and most constant care. The breach of moral trust involved in the reckless spoiling of the physical instrument of our own intellectual and spiritual life is aggravated ten-fold when we spoil the lungs or brains of those who are themselves defenceless against our rule. Moreover, to the healthy development of the child a bounding energy is needful which the adult can do without. The twelve months of over-strain or the few weeks of feverish solicitude and struggle go further towards over-balancing the poise of child-power than towards wrecking the harmonious order of a grown man's energies. Childhood is the time for *preparing* the physical instrument; in manhood, if it is simply kept in sound condition, it is enough.

But the gravity of the trust is again enormously increased when the State lays hold of the child with its all-compelling hand, and charges itself with his intellectual development. Compulsory education—however wise and necessary—is the assumption, by the State, of the responsibility inherent in the parent. The English legislature constrains the child to certain intellectual training. It is bound by every consideration alike of justice and of mercy to see to it that the form of that intellectual training shall be consonant with the best and truest physical development. It is its urgent duty to recognise the rights and functions of the body. That State which seizes the children of the poor at an age when, for the rich man's little ones, life is still but the sunny alternation between the nursery and the garden, and administers, in the name of education, a system by which the physique of multitudes is enfeebled, and preparation is made for the deterioration of the race, commits surely an almost unforgivable sin. Whosoever shall cause one of these little ones to stumble, it were better for him if a great mill-stone were hanged about his neck, and he were cast into the sea.

The path of reform, however, lies open, and there is no serious difficulty in entering on it. Let educationalists clearly expound to themselves the ideal towards which they are labouring. Is that ideal a generation of children full of useful information—information for the most part to be utterly forgotten twelve months after emancipation from the mental drill of school,—or is it a generation of bright and happy, intelligent and loving boys and girls, full of the promise of that stalwart manhood and comely womanhood which make for the greatness and virtue of a nation? The latter ideal once selected, the better way will soon be found; and the English people of the dawning twentieth century will be a people realising that noble harmony of physical and moral faculty of which Browning tells :—

> We need no longer say,
> "*Spite* of this flesh to-day,
> " I strove, made head, gained ground upon the whole."
> As a bird wings and sings,
> Let us cry, " All good things
> " Are ours, nor soul helps flesh more, now, than flesh helps soul."

LONDON:
W. SPEAIGHT AND SONS, PRINTERS, FETTER LANE.

www.ingramcontent.com/pod-product-compliance
Lightning Source LLC
Chambersburg PA
CBHW081306040426
42452CB00014B/2667

9 781535 814072